A present-day chairmaker, Stewart Linford, making Chippendale bow-back Windsor chairs, using the traditional methods of craftsmanship and producing fine chairs in the same way as in the past.

ENGLISH WINDSOR CHAIRS

Ivan G. Sparkes

Shire Publications Ltd

CONTENTS

Published in 1994 by Shire Publications Ltd, Cromwell House, Church Street, Princes Risborough, Buckinghamshire HP27 9AJ, UK. Copyright © 1981 by Ivan G. Sparkes. First published 1981, reprinted 1985, 1989 and 1994. Shire Album 70. ISBN 0 85263 562 1.

Printed in Great Britain by CIT Printing Services, Press Buildings, Merlins Bridge, Haverfordwest, Dyfed SA61 1XF.

COVER: *Edwin Skull's broadsheet, c 1863, which includes over 140 chairs of varying types, all of which were available and could be supplied at short notice.*

BELOW: *Windsor chair terms used in this book.*

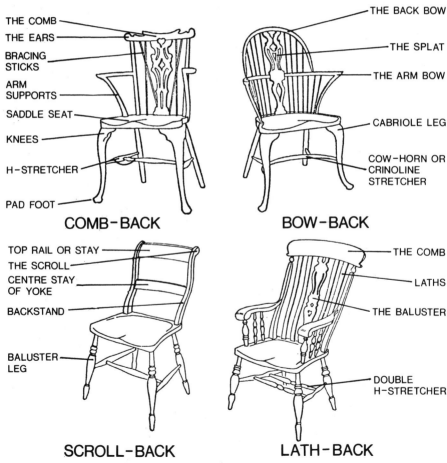

COMB-BACK

THE COMB
THE EARS
BRACING STICKS
ARM SUPPORTS
SADDLE SEAT
KNEES
H-STRETCHER
PAD FOOT

BOW-BACK

THE BACK BOW
THE SPLAT
THE ARM BOW
CABRIOLE LEG
COW-HORN OR CRINOLINE STRETCHER

SCROLL-BACK

TOP RAIL OR STAY
THE SCROLL
CENTRE STAY OF YOKE
BACKSTAND
BALUSTER LEG

LATH-BACK

THE COMB
LATHS
THE BALUSTER
DOUBLE H-STRETCHER

LEFT: *Gothic arch-back Windsor armchair with cabriole legs carved with shield-shaped knees and pierced and carved leg brackets, c 1760-70. This chair exhibits the unusual arched back, which appears very seldom in seating furniture, and here shows the figured woods used in the attractive window splats.*
RIGHT: *Early eighteenth-century comb-back with shaped comb and plain straight back splat. The legs are simply turned with a thickened cylinder turning at the point pierced by the stretcher. The stretcher itself illustrates the arrow turnings at each end of each section.*

THE COMB-BACK WINDSOR CHAIR

The Windsor chair as we know it today developed during the early years of the eighteenth century and originated in the *stick* furniture and *thrown* furniture which had for many centuries been made by the village woodturner and wheelwright. It can be easily identified by looking at the back section of the chair, as the back supports and back legs are always separated by the thickness of the seat, into which they are mortised. With most other chairs a long piece of wood, known as the backstand, forms a continuous back support and back leg into which the back edge of the seat is jointed. Many romantic theories surround the use of the term 'Windsor', which is applied to the chair, and to the idyllic sur-roundings of the beechwoods of the

Chilterns, where many millions of the nineteenth-century chairs originated.

The first recorded use of the name was in 1724 when Lord Percival's wife was carried around the grounds of Hall Barn, Buckinghamshire, 'in a Windsor chair like those at Versailles', while in 1727 John Brown, chairmaker and cabinet maker at the 'Three Covered Chair and Walnut Tree' in London, listed on his advertising card that he made 'All sorts of Windsor Garden chairs of all sizes painted green or in the wood'. Similar chairs, still painted in green, can be seen under the portico of West Wycombe Park, where they have stood since the late eighteenth century.

The earliest type of Windsor chair was probably the *comb-back*, which takes its

3

A Windsor chair is one of stick construction in which the back legs and the back supports are inserted into the upper and lower surfaces of the back part of the seat, as on the left, instead of incorporating the long floor to top rail backstand which includes both parts and is fitted to the back of the seat, as on the right.

name from the basically straight top rail out of which the sticks emerge in a fashion strongly resembling a hay rake or large comb. This was in vogue from about 1700 to 1800 and then again, in a heavier design, between about 1830 and 1920. In early chairs the comb can resemble, in a simplified form, the more elaborate crest rail of the Restoration walnut and cane chair, and it can also exhibit the use of 'ears' to terminate the comb at each side. Their shape varies from the gentle curve of the ears on the Goldsmith chair of about 1750 to the deeply carved *rosettes* on others made later in the eighteenth century.

The first examples are generally *stick-back Windsors*, which have no splat (the decorated panel in the centre of the back), and a good sturdy datable example is the Bodleian comb-back chair, introduced into the Bodleian Library at Oxford in 1766. A much more elegant comb-back with sticks is the *Goldsmith Windsor*, which belonged to the playwright Oliver Goldsmith and was presented to the Victoria and Albert Museum. This has the start of a *fan-back* (where the sticks fan outwards from the seat to a wider comb) and the legs are canted outwards at a rakish angle.

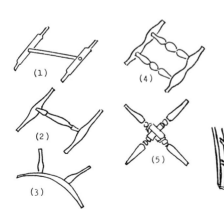

Stretchers or underframes found in Windsor and Wycombe chairs. (1) Early H stretcher. (2) Normal H stretcher. (3) Cow-horn stretcher. (4) Double H stretcher. (5) X stretcher. (6) Box stretcher.

LEFT: *Goldsmith Windsor chair of painted wood, bequeathed by Oliver Goldsmith in 1774 to William Hawes MD and then presented to the Victoria and Albert Museum.*
RIGHT: *Goldsmith-type Windsor chair with shield-shaped seat, c 1770. This has a built-up arm bow in three parts, joined at the back, instead of the usual bent member, and the arms lie well back from the front of the seat.*

The Windsor chair, like much country furniture, has been influenced over the centuries by other, more fashionable designs. Richly ornamented examples include the seven japanned Windsor chairs which the Duke of Chandos had for his library at Cannons in 1725 and the carved mahogany chairs reported to have been made for the library of the Prince of Wales about 1730. The designs of Chippendale influenced some beautifully produced and finished late eighteenth-century Windsor chairs (1770-1800) with the typical Chippendale cupid's bow crest rail, carved with shells and wheat husks, standing on cabriole legs with well carved knees and strengthened with attractively curved spur stretchers (also know as crinoline or cow-horn stretchers).

The most unusual of the eighteenth-century chairs, which appears as a bow-back or as an arched back, is linked to the Gothic Revival of the later eighteenth century, and it bears such names as the Strawberry Hill, Gothic or church-window splat Windsor. It uses three open tracery splats in place of the back sticks of earlier chairs and has one smaller splat on each side also, infilling the arm supports, all echoing the tracery of stone Gothic church windows, giving a richness to the design. This is given even greater emphasis when these window splats are enclosed in an arch-shaped back bow. The Gothic Windsor had quite a short life (c 1755-70) but has been revived since the Second World War and is gaining popularity in a specialised way. To many, its eccentric lines are totally alien to the simplicity of the country wheel-back in the same way that many will not accept the cabriole leg as being in sympathy with the rest of the Windsor chair's design.

Other versions of the comb-back include the *fan-back Windsor,* where the comb, which is rather wider than the width of the seat, enables the sticks to fan out in an attractive manner. This is most noticeable

5

ABOVE LEFT: *Windsor fan-back armchair with Chippendale comb and splat, cabriole legs and an H stretcher with arrow turnings in the central stretcher piece; a rather heavy looking chair with the arms clumsily designed, c 1770-1800.*

ABOVE RIGHT: *Mid eighteenth-century fan-back Windsor side chair with Chippendale splat, a bobtail and bracing sticks. The stretcher has the arrow turning in the central stretcher piece.*

BELOW LEFT: *Sturdy eighteenth-century comb-back with fiddle-back splat. The use of four cabriole legs is not unusual but makes the chair look heavier in design, but this is relieved by the beautifully carved shells on the knees of the front cabriole legs and the attractive scroll in the ears of the well-shaped comb.*

BELOW RIGHT: *Early comb-back Windsor armchair with fiddle-back splat and shell ornament and pronounced ears in the curved comb. The cabriole legs show its early design: they are very straight and hardly balance the proportions of the seat and upper parts. About 1740.*

in the side chair, but it is also present in the armchair of the Chippendale style. Another unusual variant is the *shawl-back;* here the comb is sharply curved forward on either end, enabling a shawl to be thrown over the chair to form an alcove against draughts. A few examples of the scarcer *balloon-back* are found from time to time; in this type the comb is either considerably narrower than the seat width or is replaced by a half-circular disc into which the sticks, as they are socketed, bend inwards giving a similar effect to that of the *Shetland chair.*

The legs in early examples of the rural chairs were often shaved with a spokeshave rather than turned on a lathe, and as a stretcher was not always used the legs stand stoutly, angled well outwards to withstand the downward pressure when in use. Such shaved legs appear in England in chairs of the early to mid eighteenth century, but in Wales they can be much later, even into the early nineteenth century. In time the legs would be turned, and certainly chairs from the 1740s onwards had turned legs, but the shaved leg in England lasted until the 1770s, with the cabriole leg in use throughout the eighteenth century. The turned leg in the eighteenth century incorporated the vase turning but with the emphasis on the lower part of the legs, as with the Goldsmith chair, but between 1770 and 1790 the turning began to change to the more familiar slim baluster leg of the classic Windsor chair, with ring, ball and vase and a high bulge in the vase shape.

The cabriole leg, introduced by 1725-30 in the Windsor chair, was in vogue until about 1810 and was a survival from the furniture of the Queen Anne era. It used the hoof foot in many places, and also the pad foot (most popular in present-day cabriole legs) and the claw and ball in fine examples. Usually only the front legs were cabriole, with the back legs simply turned, or even plain, and slanted back at a sharp angle for stability. Some mid eighteenth-century Windsor chairs were made with four cabriole legs, and they tend to look rather square, showing a William Kent influence, and seem somewhat uncompromising. The use of the cabriole in place of the baluster legs is often considered to be out of character with the chair, but with a well carved leg, carved bracket and pad foot it can appear very effective.

The early chairs frequently had no stretcher, but the cabriole-legged chairs used the cow-horn or spur stretcher, which consists of a curved bow-like stretcher linking the front legs, from which two spurs or turned spindles project to connect with the back legs. This is an elegant alternative to the more familiar H stretcher, and it is occasionally found in chairs in the form of a double cow-horn or serpentine X stretcher. The height of the eighteenth-century stretcher is usually midway between the seat and the floor, while the nineteenth-century stretcher moved down lower in the first half of the century, until it was fitted about 9 inches to 1 foot (230 to 305 mm) from the ground. In the mid twentieth century it rose again and now stands about 4 inches (100 mm) below the seat in extreme examples.

Windsor chairs are traditionally made of beech, but this is usually confined to turned parts, with the seats being made of elm and the bent parts of ash, yew or fruitwood. The elm seat is square in basic shape and shield shape in detail, with the exception of some northern chairs whose seats tend to be wider than they are deep. The grain runs normally from front to back, except in the wide chairs, and chairs up to the 1890s were almost certainly all adzed to obtain the saddle effect on the upper surface, called *bottoming.* Some early chairs also have the underside adzed instead of sawn, but after the introduction of the steam-saw mill in factories the underside was usually only sawn and received no further treatment. The under rim of the chair is sometimes chamfered or shaved to conform with the upper curves of the bottoming, a feature noticeable in late eighteenth-century and mid twentieth-century examples.

The sticks themselves are usually simply turned rods. When they have a slight swell about a third of the way up they are called *spindles.* In later chairs (c 1850) they can be found decorated with rings and turned shapes, and these might be called *Roman spindles.* Again with some early or crude examples, the sticks may be shaved rather than turned, and when they were turned on the pole lathe a special rest had to be used to stop them *whipping* as the chisel was used to cut their shape. The most effective part of the Windsor chair is the ornamental

Comb-back chairs. (From left to right, top row) Early type of Windsor comb-back, eighteenth century; comb-back with cabriole legs, early to mid eighteenth century; fan-back side chair, c 1750; Bodleian fan-back side chair, c 1780. (Middle row) Bodleian comb-back, 1766; wide comb-back Windsor, mid eighteenth century; balloon-back Windsor, c 1780; Goldsmith Windsor, mid eighteenth century. (Bottom row) Slim comb-back, late eighteenth century; Mendlesham regional Windsor, c 1790-1830; shawl-back Windsor, late eighteenth century; Chippendale comb-back, c 1770-1800.

RIGHT: *The Bodleian comb-back, which was introduced into the Bodleian Library, Oxford, in 1766. The legs are still unturned, and the design has a country look about it in comparison with the more lavish Windsor designs of the eighteenth century.*

BELOW LEFT: *Shawl-back Windsor chair, late eighteenth century, with deeply curved comb carved from a block of wood instead of being steam-bent. This chair has a classic vase in the splat, and the high back is designed to take a shawl or covering to create a draught-proof shelter.*

BELOW RIGHT: *Balloon-back Windsor chair, late eighteenth century. The comb, which is less wide than the seat, forces the back sticks inward, giving the chair its balloon effect.*

9

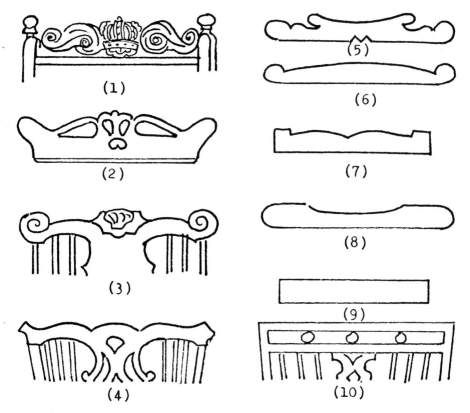

Examples of cresting rails and combs found in the comb-back Windsor chair. (1) Cresting rail of Restoration cane chair, c 1680. (2) Comb of the barley sugar Windsor chair, c 1680. (3) Comb of Parker Knoll Collection Windsor, c 1740. (4) Comb of Chippendale Windsor, 1770-1810. (5) Fan-back, c 1750. (6) Comb from the Goldsmith chair, c 1750. (7) Comb from Bodleian fan-back single chair, c 1770. (8) Comb from Bodleian Library Windsor, c 1766. (9) Final form of the comb, early nineteenth century. (10) Top rail of the Mendlesham chair, c 1820.

splat or wooden vertical rail in the back of the chair, which is also called the baluster. This does not appear to have been introduced until the 1720s, when the unpierced *fiddle-back* or *Hogarth* shape came into use. The vase or urn shape within a circle has a classic connotation linked with the Adam designs of the classic style of the 1760s, while the Prince of Wales feathers, another popular motif, might well be associated with Hepplewhite's use of this familiar royal badge in the backs of his chairs while under the patronage of the Prince of Wales. Other designs incorporate the wheel (to be discussed later), the disc (or draught), the cross, the crown or the star.

The comb-back Windsor dropped out of fashion in the late eighteenth century, in the face of the growing popularity of the bow-back, and it was not until the 1830s and 1840s that it returned to the scene in the form of the spindle-back and lath-back of the Victorian period.

LEFT: *Gothic window-splat bow-back Windsor armchair with crinoline stretcher, c 1775. These chairs, made for only a few decades, reflect the interest in antiquarian architecture at the time.* RIGHT: *Stick-back Windsor chair, c 1790, of common design, but rather elegant in the way it has been produced. The legs show the early use of the classic baluster leg with its slim swell between the top and bottom turnings, while the proportions generally seem just right.*

THE BOW-BACK WINDSOR CHAIR

It was a short step to develop the comb-back into the bow-back once the principle of bending the arm bow was understood, and it seems that the back bow came into use about 1740. It provided a sturdier back support than the comb and also reduced the amount of work in finishing off the back of the chair. As with the comb-back, the earlier examples seem to have been of the stick-back variety, and then, following the popularity of the ornamental splat in the comb-back, this was soon brought into use with the bow-back. Very quickly the bow-back adopted the Gothic style between the 1750s and 1770s and so became a suitable basis for the use of equally elaborate splats by the great designers. Mahogany bow-back chairs, such as the shell chair of the Parker Knoll Collection, have the pierced splat delicately carved with wheatears, husks and rosettes, while the Chippendale *riband splat,* which appears so successfully in his 'Director' of

1754, occurs in a simplified version which has remained in demand into the twentieth century, as it matches in so well with the cabriole leg and the more finely finished effects of the Chippendale bowback.

As elegant in style were the results of the attempt to revive designs during the Regency period. They show a more scholarly use of the classic motifs of the period, in particular the introduction of the single bow-back armchair, also called the loop-back, which spanned the Regency period (*c* 1810-20), where the arms were mortised into the sides of the back bow instead of using an arm bow. The use of the triple splat with ogee piercing or the Prince of Wales feathers is very reminiscent of the triple splats seen in the backs of the Hepplewhite chairs. Typical of Sheraton's influence on the Windsor is the interlaced bow, which remained in the catalogues until the 1870s; there are at least three variants of this.

ABOVE LEFT: *Triple-splat Windsor single-bow armchair, c 1800, with Prince of Wales feathers motif in the splats; the unusual arm splats are each pierced with the same motif.*
ABOVE RIGHT: *Chippendale bow-back Windsor chair, late eighteenth century, with low cabriole legs and well turned back legs. The front feet are pad feet and lifted well off the ground.*
BELOW LEFT: *Triple-splat Windsor single-bow armchair, c 1800, with ogee piercings in the splats and arrow turnings in the H stretcher. The centre splat is designed to rise with the bow, a point of good craftsmanship.*
BELOW RIGHT: *Mahogany bow-back, late eighteenth century, its pierced splay delicately carved with wheatears, husks and rosettes. Of particular interest is the X stretcher linking the legs.*

Two Prince of Wales feathers Windsor side chairs, possibly c 1820-40. The chair on the left uses the triple ring in the leg, which in later years was an identifying feature of chairs made in the Chilterns.

THE WHEEL-BACK WINDSOR CHAIR

The introduction of the wheel motif into the bow-back splat provided the impetus to make the bow-back, or the wheel-back as it became known, the most popular of all chair designs. The dating of the wheel is uncertain, but Dr John Stabler's research has proved its use about 1780 following the discovery of an inscription written in ink on the underside of a wheel-back: 'Mr Longridge, Gateshead, Durham, 6 chairs by the *Vulcan*, Capt R. Hawks or by the first ship in that trade.' This narrowed the date down to c 1779-83.

Once established, the wheel-back Windsor chair in its various forms has gone from strength to strength, accounting for at least seventy-five per cent of all Windsor chairs produced over the past 150 years. The number made is enormous: High Wycombe alone in the 1860s produced almost five thousand chairs a day in the town and its environs. The popularity of the Windsor chair is shown in Loudon's *Encyclopedia* of 1833, where he writes that it was 'one of the best kitchen chairs in general use in the Midland counties of England'.

The basic design has remained constant

Bow-back designs. (From left to right, top row) Wheel-back side chair, early design c 1750; stick-back Windsor chair, c 1790; Gothic Windsor with arch bow, c 1750-70; Chippendale bow-back by Jack Goodchild, c 1950. (Middle row) Single-bow Windsor of interlaced bow type, c 1790-1820; typical wheel-back Windsor, c 1780 to date; triple-splat Hepplewhite Windsor, c 1840. (Bottom row) Low-back Windsor made in Nottinghamshire, c 1840; two versions of the Lancashire style Windsor, also made in Nottinghamshire as a high-back Windsor.

LEFT: *Windsor single-bow wheel-back armchair, c 1820, of simple clean design. The stretcher shows how the sharper arrow turnings in the stretchers of the earlier chairs are losing their crispness and will soon give way to simpler curved turnings.*

RIGHT: *Wheel-back Windsor chair with cut-down legs, making it a nursing chair. Probably c 1820-30, this chair shows the increasing height of the bow, which is characteristic of the period.*

over this period and so it is the finer points which help to make dating possible. The bows of the early chairs tend to be slender and rounded on the outer edge, but by the 1860s they seem to be thicker and of square section. The older chairs or the individually made wheel-backs have the seat heavily saddled and the under edge chamfered to give the effect of slimness, and the cutting away of the centre of the seat brings the thickness of the plank from its uncut 2 inches (50 mm) down to almost ¾ inch (19 mm). The legs too have significant features in their turnings. The use of the triple ring is quite late, possibly not earlier than 1880, and it has a strong link with chairs made in High Wycombe. The classic baluster leg has itself changed over the centuries, and the slender high bulge of the chair legs of the late eighteenth century to the early nineteenth century developed so that the swell in the vase shape became more and more pronounced

until by the 1870s what was termed the *piano leg* was in vogue, with the rather complicated ball and ring arrangement above the vase, a very long tapered shank which pierced the chair seat and a foot taper at least 4 inches (100 mm) long before the first ring. This foot taper is a straight and slender taper until about 1870 and since 1910, but for the period in between it is frequently turned with a strong swell immediately below the ring. This takes away much of the elegance of the chair and goes by the name *tulip* or *onion foot*.

The cow-horn stretcher was in use up to the Regency period, when it gave way in popularity in many instances to the H stretcher, which was more acceptable for the new generation of baluster leg chairs. This H stretcher gradually evolved over the years, and examples of the mid eighteenth century had a simple turning in the centre of the cross and side parts of the stretcher

15

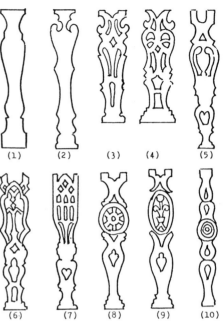

ABOVE LEFT: *Triple-splat Windsor side chair, c 1840, with a turned disc in the centre of each of the three pierced splats, a bobtail extension to the seat and bracing sticks. This chair has 'Hepplewhite' features.*

ABOVE RIGHT: *Splats or balusters used in Windsor chairs. (1 and 2) Early eighteenth-century unpierced 'vase' splats. (3) Chippendale splat, c 1770. (4) Development of Chippendale splat, somewhat later. (5) Classical urn or vase splat, c 1770-1820. (6 and 7) Gothic splats, c 1750-70. (8) Wheel-back splat, c 1820 to date. (9) Prince of Wales feathers splat, c 1790-1830. (10) Blind wheel or disc splat, c 1820-30.*

LEFT: *Interlaced bow, Gothic style Windsor side chair, c 1820, a narrow chair with a small seat, rather square in shape.*

with the sides of the cross stretcher swelling out each end into an arrow taper, so narrowing down to the point where they mortise into the side stretchers. This stretcher lost its decorative turnings by the 1760s, these being replaced by a swell in the centre of each section. The swell and taper on the cross section remained until about 1820 when all three parts of the H stretcher reverted to the single swell in the centre of each.

Interlaced bow, Gothic style Windsor single-bow back armchair, c 1820. One of several interlaced bow designs found in chairs of this period.

Two Windsor scroll-back side chairs. (Right) A plain splat type, c 1865. (Left) A Gothic side chair with the arched upper and lower stays linked with baluster-turned spindles, c 1840-60.

THE SCROLL-BACK AND ITS VARIETIES

A fundamental change in the shape of the Windsor chair took place by the 1830s. In Loudon's *Encyclopedia* of 1833 the wheel-back chair and what is now termed the *scroll-back* are lauded. The latter was described as a very comfortable and cheap chair. The design is vastly different from former styles, as the bow and sticks are discarded, and the back has no comb. Instead, the main feature lies in the shape of the two sturdy *backstands* or uprights, which are 'scrolled over', i.e. curved backwards at the top, standing just proud of the top rail, which has now superseded the comb. This style is also called the *stay-back* Windsor, taking its name from the turned and shaped stay which forms the central member across the back of the chair. The design gives us a strong link with the Regency period and exhibits the attractive lines which are reminiscent of the fashionable eighteenth-century dining room chairs. The height is reduced, so it presents a neater and more conservative piece of furniture than the traditional Windsor, without any loss in comfort. As a ladies' chair it was made in a slimmer model, waisted into a smaller seat, and by the use of many different *yoke rails* or *back stays* a wide range of chairs in this design was created.

The *Gothic* scroll-back has circular arches cut into the top rail which are supported by turned spindles which act as miniature pillars, linking the top rail to the

RIGHT: *Scroll-back Windsor side chair, c 1865, with plain angled central stay flanked by double bobbin turnings each side. The seat is well chamfered in the underside to reduce its apparent thickness when seen from above, and it has well turned baluster legs with simple and crisp turnings.*

BELOW LEFT: *Buckle-back Windsor side chair, c 1875. Here the central stay is ornamented with pierced pattern work, which in elaborate examples resembles a belt buckle. The backstands are of square section and have two grooves made with scratch tools.*

BELOW RIGHT: *Twisted scroll Windsor side chair with triple ring turnings in the legs and tulip turning at the feet. The central stay has a rope-like effect with the twisted barley sugar turning and is flanked by baluster turnings. The stay is reputed to commemorate the death of Nelson in 1812. The chair can be dated as c 1845.*

ABOVE LEFT: *Scroll-back Windsor mess armchair with one arm, c 1890. Such chairs were made for use in the army, this one for Preston Barracks.*

ABOVE RIGHT: *Stephen Hazell Windsor chair, c 1860, with tablet back, diagonal back stays crowned with a ring where they intersect each other.*

LEFT: *Stephen Hazell Windsor scroll-back, c 1865, with the cyma curved arms linked by turned balusters to the seat.*

yoke rail. These chairs are also called *spindle Gothics* and in the High Wycombe price lists sold at 32s a dozen in the 1860s. When the yoke rail was elaborately carved it created the *buckle-back* and when the yoke rail was cut into a rope-like finish it became the *twisted scroll*, sometimes called the *Nelson* or the *Trafalgar scroll-back*. The latter names come from the sea rope being associated with the death of Nelson at Trafalgar in

1805, and the furniture produced after his death was called Trafalgar furniture. A more unusual variety has a crossed diagonal X stay in the back, with a flat horizontal panel replacing the top rail and scroll finials; this has Sheraton elements in its design and is called a *tablet-back*, the name being the cabinet maker's term for a flat writing surface.

One of the identifiable makers of the scroll-back was Stephen Hazell of Oxford, working c 1846-69. He brought to the scroll-back several features which were quickly adopted by the other manufacturers. A striking departure from the traditional stay came with his use of the diagonal back stays in the form of an X, decorated with a small ring centred over the junction. Another way in which many of his chairs are recognisable is the way in which the arms curve downwards to the seat in a cyma curve, linked to the seat with a turned spindle, a style similar to the Sheraton chair. Hazell is one of the few Windsor chairmakers who stamped his chairs, and a 'signed Hazell' is a worthwhile investment.

An unusual scroll-back made about 1890 was the one-armed mess chair, in which the absence of the left arm enabled the dress sword to hang from the waist of the soldier, unencumbered, so that when he rose to a toast he could do so without any complications or entanglements. Two such chairs are in the Wycombe Chair Museum, believed to have been made for the officers' mess at Preston Barracks.

Most scroll-backs can be dated to between 1840 and 1935, with the plainer designs lasting the whole period, the Gothic types c 1840-70, the twisted scroll c 1840-70, the tablet-back c 1860, the buckle-backs c 1860-90, and the one-armed mess chairs c 1890-1910.

SPINDLE-BACK AND LATH-BACK WINDSOR CHAIRS

A further distinctive change took place in the design of the Windsor chair about 1840 when the *Wycombe style* Windsor chair came on the scene. It heralded the return of the comb-back, but the comb in question was extremely heavy in design and up to 6 inches (150 mm) in depth, modelled in the pear-top shape. The chair was also higher than most previous styles, in direct contrast to the scroll-back, which was developing at the same time. In its first form, the *spindle-back*, the sticks in the back were spindles which were simply turned and given a swell about a third of the way up. This offered some slight support to the small of the back and so added to the comfort of the user. As with the single-bow and the scroll-back, the arms of the spindle-back Windsor are mortised into the backstands, and with cheaper models they are flat and terminate rather abruptly but with better models the hand rests are scrolled over. The H stretcher, which at first was well proportioned, in time became thicker, as the chair's legs grew shorter and more heavily turned. They took on a second cross member and so became *double H stretchers*, with the side members of the stretcher growing so solid as to be termed *sausage stretchers*. The spindles in the back were also by the 1850s fully turned with swells, rings and suchlike and their use created the *Roman spindle Windsor*.

Whilst shaped spindles were a concession to comfort, they made little allowance for the true shape of the human spine and so a curved lath was introduced by the early 1850s to replace them. These laths were of flat rectangular section and were shaped, together with the backstands and the splat, to curve more strongly so that the whole shape of the chair was designed around this new concept. The lath-back Windsor chair was made in several forms, and the principle of the pear-drop comb and the curved laths was carried over into folding chairs, producing very elaborate deck or steamer chairs, which preceded the modern metal and canvas deckchair. The prices for these Wycombe Windsor chairs in 1872 were, by modern ¹ standards, modest: lath armchair 9s; lath and baluster armchair 15s; rocking chair 19s; side chairs 54s a

LEFT: *Wycombe Windsor lath-back armchair, c 1890, showing the very heavily turned baluster legs with their mushroom turnings and the tulip turnings in the feet. The use of the laths in the back of the chair offered greater comfort, and the heavier chair so produced required a double-H stretcher for strength. The sausage turnings in the side pieces of the stretcher serve to give thickness to accept the centre stretcher parts inserted into them.*

RIGHT: *Windsor spindle-back armchair, c 1875, with triple ring in the legs and strong swell in the turnings of the back spindles. This chair, which is a throwback to the comb-back chairs, probably preceded the lath-back Windsor chairs.*

dozen.

When the decorative splat in the back was reintroduced to the lath-back it became a *lath and baluster chair*, and in a very large version at the Wycombe Chair Museum the splat carries the monogram of the owner. Other Windsor chairs which evolved out of the lath-back included the *Swiss chair*, in which some similarity to the Swiss or Austrian folk style was introduced. The top rail or comb is shaped, sometimes having the pointed tops of the backstands poking through, while the sticks or spindles in the back and sides are replaced by lengths of intertwined cane. The dating of this chair is difficult, but probably *c* 1840-80.

The lath-back style of Windsor chair was a very popular country chair, known as a *farmhouse Windsor*, its very solidness and strength appealing to cottagers and working class buyers. It survived the

Edwardian period and was manufactured well into the 1920s, at a time when the heavier Windsors seem to have been overtaken by the low-back types.

Roman spindle Windsor side chair, c 1890. When the spindle in the back of the chair was turned with ornamentation, it was called a Roman spindle.

22

RIGHT: *Spindle-back Windsor side chair made for military use in 1917. It has very crudely turned legs, with only a plain ring top and bottom to reduce the turning time, and a solid, very shallow-saddled seat, to keep the costs down. But, for strength in the barracks, an extra stretcher has been inserted to link the lower part of the back legs.*

BELOW LEFT: *Fine Wycombe Windsor lath and baluster armchair, c 1890, with the initials of the owner, HT (Harry Towerton of Stokenchurch, Buckinghamshire) in the decorated splat. These chairs are also called farmhouse Windsor chairs.*

BELOW RIGHT: *Lath and baluster Windsor rocking chair, late nineteenth or early twentieth century, with solidly turned legs and a very simply pierced splat. It has been fitted with rockers, and these could be attached to almost any chair at the request of the customer.*

ABOVE: *Eighteenth-century Windsor comb-back settee from Jesus College, Oxford. This is a two-seater version, with the comb clearly defined and the bottoming of the seat separated into two sections.*

TOP RIGHT: *Nineteenth-century three-legged Windsor stool with Isle of Man stretcher. This is very similar to stools illustrated in the catalogues of the 1860s.*

CENTRE RIGHT: *Eighteenth-century Windsor stool with cabriole leg, cow-horn stretcher and deeply saddled seat. Note the use of the cabriole leg in the front for stability, also the turnings on the single spur section of the stretcher.*

RIGHT: *Swiss style Windsor armchair with twisted cane replacing the usual sticks or laths in the arms and the back, c 1860. The splat bears the cut-out symbol VA and a crown, commemorating Queen Victoria and Prince Albert.*

A Windsor Gothic yew, elm and beechwood triple-back settee, c 1750-1800, from the collection of the late Benjamin Sonnenberg. This appears to be a very clear match to the Gothic armchair in the Victoria and Albert Museum, and it shows the use of the bracket at the top of the cabriole leg.

WINDSOR ROCKING CHAIRS, SETTEES AND STOOLS

The rocking chair, although accepted in the eighteenth century in America, did not gain favour in England until the nineteenth century, and even then only on medical grounds. Dr Calvert recommended it as a digestive chair, helpful to invalids and members of the weaker sex. In High Wycombe Benjamin North was making the 'American rocking chair' in the 1850s, but earlier, in Loudon's *Encyclopedia* of 1838, are included notes on two rocking chairs. The Skull catalogue of 1849 includes several Windsor chairs mounted on rockers, and the practice of providing rockers of different lengths, which could be fitted to almost any desired chair, was a standard practice in the 1870s. Rocker-mounted Windsor chairs are scarce, so it may be that they were less durable than the standard chair or less popular than other types of rocker.

During the mid eighteenth century, with the growth in popularity of the settee and sofa and the hall settee, some very fine examples of Windsor settees were designed. The most common method was to produce a two or three seater settee, created by linking the back designs of fashionable chairs such as the Gothic Windsor, and make it to match as a set the armchairs of the same pattern. But also made were some impressive settees with a continuous comb, such as the example at Jesus College, Oxford, and in the United States a wide variety were made for places of worship.

Eighteenth-century Windsor stools have a remarkable elegance, while those of the nineteenth century are as varied in design as the uses to which they were put. An interesting survival is the three-legged version, *c* 1870, in the Wycombe Chair Museum, which exhibits the symmetrical Isle of Man stretcher bracing the sturdy legs.

LEFT: *Bergere bow Windsor armchair, a style of High Victorian low-back used in offices and public buildings, frequently with a swivel base instead of standard legs; c 1850-70.*
RIGHT: *Mahogany baluster-back library chair, c 1730. Note the crisp carving on the scroll at the back of the arm bow, on the arm supports and the knees of the cabriole legs. These were the forerunners of the nineteenth-century smoker's bow chairs.*

THE LOW-BACK WINDSOR CHAIR

The *low-back Windsor* is usually considered to be a mid nineteenth-century innovation, but its origin can be traced back to the Queen Anne style writing chair of the early eighteenth century. Similar chairs, specifically in a Windsor style of construction, were developing in America and the Philadelphia low-back of 1725 was remodelled to become the *smoker's bow* by the 1820s. This is the type of low-back which came to England soon after, for although it is not represented in Loudon's *Encyclopedia* of 1833 it is in Edwin Skull's catalogue of 1847 and so was probably introduced about 1840.

The *smoker's bow* is the most popular of the low-backs and still exists in great numbers around the British countryside. The seat section is traditional, with heavy baluster legs and a single or double H stretcher. The upper section consists of a continuous arm bow with outward flaring arm finials supported by two heavy and usually seven lesser turned spindles. The back upper side of the arm bow is sur-

mounted by a very deep backward rolled scroll. As with the wheel-back, the basic design of this chair has not changed in 150 years, and only the use of sticks or spats instead of turned spindles or a change in design of the back scroll can help in determining their age. The Skull catalogue of 1847 contains two models, one the traditional smoker's bow with H stretcher, five turned spindles, wooden seat and the very heavy piano legs of the period. The other model has an elaborately pierced central splat, side splats replacing the arm supports, a cane seat and the curved back which later developed into the *bergere bow*.

The smoker's bow was used in offices, public buildings, library reading rooms, barbers' shops, restaurants and public houses, and it was in constant demand from the 1840s through to the 1930s. It has, since the end of the Second World War, become popular once more and is produced in several forms, being used extensively as a kindergarten chair for young children.

26

The three basic types of low-back Windsor armchairs: (from left) the smoker's bow, the firehouse Windsor, the captain's chair.

The *firehouse Windsor* was another development in the low-back style and was produced in the United States between 1850 and 1870. It takes its name from its frequent use by the volunteer fire companies of the nineteenth century. It differs from the *smoker's bow* in having a *box stretcher*, that is one which goes around the four chair legs rather than crossing between them. It has also a much slimmer arm bow, which ends abruptly where the hands rest, having no outward flair. The firehouse Windsor was in use in England by the 1850s and was described as 'a neat and satisfactory dining room seat for a cottage'. It appears in the Walter Ellis catalogue of *c* 1870 with eight spindles, the seat cut with a serpentine shaped front edge and the familiar cut-out hand grip in the low back cresting.

Next came the *captain's chair, c* 1865-80, used initially in the pilot houses of the Mississippi river steamers. The box stretcher is again used, and the arm bow curves downwards to be socketed into the seat. It often has a ply seat insert with holes punched in a regular design or in a floral pattern.

These three low-back Windsor chairs are essentially American in design but found favour in England, where they were made for over a century. Much more English in spirit are the Victorian curves of the *bergere bow*. This has a very high curved back with the arms flamboyantly scrolled over, supported by spindles or splats, and dates from about 1860 to 1890. These low-back chairs appear in various forms in the catalogues of the 1860s and 1870s and Glenister's catalogue of *c* 1860 includes twelve different priced types, with

the smoker's bow ranging from 10s with a wooden seat to 30s in mahogany with a cane seat, and the bergere bow at 14s with a wooden seat to 35s for a revolving office type in mahogany.

The classic smoker's bow Windsor armchair, as used in offices, public buildings, hotels and reading rooms from the mid nineteenth century into the 1930s.

LEFT: *Unusual Lancashire Windsor armchair, c 1825, fitted with a double bow which surmounts the back bow. This was a feature in American Windsor chairs, but it is very rare indeed on English Windsors.*

RIGHT: *Mendlesham chair of Windsor style construction, c 1820. This example has turned sticks in the back, a feature not always found in this type of chair, and also incorporates the bent stay and wooden balls. The legs have a different form of swell turning which is more angular than in traditional baluster legs.*

REGIONAL WINDSOR CHAIRS
AND CHILDREN'S CHAIRS

Over the years Windsor chairs developed in three main groups: firstly, the traditional designs, which appear to be common to all areas; secondly, the manufacturers' chairs, which in the nineteenth century were geared to catalogues and were standardised to a considerable extent; and thirdly, the regional chairs, which can often be recognised and assigned to a particular region or town from some special identifying factor.

Among the earlier regional styles is the *Cardiganshire chair* from Wales. There are both three-legged and four-legged varieties and they bear a strong resemblance to the cruder Windsor chairs of the early eighteenth century, though they were produced at a later date. The use of three legs gives stability on uneven floors and

could well have been essential in cottages and farmhouses. The construction included an extra thick *plank seat* made of elm or bog-oak, cut roughly into a D shape. The curved line at the back is followed by an equally heavy-looking arm bow with a roughly finished scroll and outward flaring arms. The spindles were made of beech or birch and these date from the mid eighteenth century.

There is no roughness or country look about the East Anglian Windsor chair which appeared in the early years of the nineteenth century, known as the *Mendlesham chair*. It is a stylish variety of the single-bow Windsor armchair, but with the back bow replaced by a square back rail and straight backstands, not resembling the bow or comb in any way. The chair is reputed to have originated in the village of Mendlesham in Suffolk and is linked with the local wheelwright and chairmaker Daniel Day. Not many examples exist today, and they are usually made of yew or fruitwood with an elm saddled seat. The back design includes a Regency-style copy of the ornamental splat in miniature, with three angled sticks each side, surmounted by a double crest rail of square section, in-filled with turned wooden balls. Different chairs include the use of curved rails below the splat section, and all examples exhibit an elegance not wholly expected in a Windsor-type chair.

Much heavier in design is the *Lancashire* or *Yorkshire* Windsor chair, which is more sturdily constructed than the normal Windsor and is often called a *high-back* Windsor, because of the height of the back bow. This bow differs from that of the traditional Windsor, as it springs from the arm bow in a much more dramatic way, with the thickness of the upper section of the bow

(usually made of yew) shaved down to the point where the two sides enter the arm bow. The splat is also usually in two parts, separated by the arm bow, not like the long continuous splat of the traditional Windsor, which is inset into the front of the arm bow. Although the sticks in some versions pierce the arm bow and so stretch from the seat to the back bow, in others they are limited to the upper section of the chair, and the arm bow is linked to the seat by a row of turned spindles. Some of the original northern chairs may have come south; most of the Lancashires found in the Home Counties tend to be dated *c* 1820-60 and they were, more often than not, made in the smaller workshops of the north. After this period heavier turnings became more popular, and Lancashire chairs were made successfully in the Chilterns for the London and northern markets.

Another northern chair, known as the *low bow-back* Windsor, can be identified with the area of Yorkshire called Rockley,

LEFT: *Lancashire type regional Windsor armchair, c 1825, with the high bow and separated splat, typical of this type of chair.*
RIGHT: *Rockley made Windsor child's low chair, c 1865, with a low curve to the back bow, otherwise similar to the Lancashire model. Rockley chairs are often stamped with the maker's name, which makes them more collectable.*

where a colony of chairmakers thrived between 1825 and 1865, with Frederick Walker, William Wheatland and George Nicholson stamping their chairs for identification. Others worked in nearby Worksop and Wellow. As in the Chiltern area, they later worked on a larger scale, producing in 1870 six basic designs; by 1900 this had risen to twenty-seven chair patterns. Their *smoking high Windsor* was similar to the Lancashire version, but their *best-low Windsor* is a style with which the Rockley chairs are more closely identified. Here the bow is quite low, the splat split by the arm bow, and often the upper section is shorter in height than the lower part between the arm bow and the seat. As with the Lancashire, a thick bow, tapered slightly where it enters the arm bow, is a feature one finds, giving a pleasant sturdiness to the design.

A child's version, stamped *Walker/Rockley*, in the Wycombe Chair Museum shows the way in which children's

furniture in the past was produced with the same precision, design and durability as the adult chairs. Many of the surviving children's chairs are high chairs, often dating from the 1820s, and they have their own elegance. They are often produced as bow-back or scroll-back chairs, using splats cut with the wheel, urn, Prince of Wales feathers or disc. These long-legged versions were difficult to design, and although most exhibit a perfect sense of proportion, sometimes one finds the lower leg section heavier in design than acceptable, indicating that they may well have been adapted rather than designed. Surviving high chairs are frequently lacking their foot rests and the wooden pegs which supported them, and the holes left gaping or blocked with dowels show the way in which the foot rest could be lowered as the child grew larger and outgrew his chair. The holes bored through the arms secured the restraining bar which stopped the struggling infant from falling to the ground.

LEFT: *Child's Windsor disc-back high chair with both footrest and restraining bar in position; early nineteenth century.*

RIGHT: *Bergere bow Windsor child's high chair, c 1860. This chair shows how the use of unmatched parts in the lower section can produce an ungainly chair.*

MODERN WINDSOR FURNITURE

The tradition of the bodger working in the woods began to decline before the mechanisation and modernisation of the furniture industry at the beginning of the twentieth century. The role of the bodger diminished in the face of rising prices, so that by the beginning of the Second World War (1939) only a few were still working in the Chilterns. One or two firms in the 1930s were still faithful, 'not because of any sentimental reason to try and keep an ancient craft going, but because it could in some instances be economic', as the old bodger could turn out chair legs more quickly and far better than the best up-to-date automatic machinery of that time. In the Wycombe area in the post-war period Samuel Rockall lived and worked in Turville in Buckinghamshire, and the brothers Owen and George Dean were two other chairmakers, working in Hampden Woods on the outskirts of Wycombe. Perhaps the best known of the Chiltern rural chairmakers was Jack Goodchild, whose work is prized and valued in a way usually reserved for antique furniture. He pursued his craft from the turning of the legs to the finishing of the chair.

By contrast, in 1937 Harry Hopkins wrote about 'Lucian Ercolani . . . the *enfant terrible* of High Wycombe's mass-production revolution, the "Ford" of the Windsor chair'. This was an unfortunate description, for while the concept of Ercol Limited goes a long way on the path to mass-production it still retains much of the craftsman's oversight and finish, continuing the tradition in the form of a machine-aided craft. The firm of Ercol did much to revitalise the Windsor chair and, even more important, created a whole range of kitchen, dining room and sitting room furniture which matched it in both materials and design, making the rural chair much more an integral part of modern furniture than it ever was in the past. In Ercol's new designs Lucian Ercolani retained the elements of the traditional Windsor chair, but he lifted the stretcher height, reduced or eliminated the decorative turning in the legs, allowed the clean lines of the timbers to be seen and enabled the eighteenth-century Windsor chair to survive without stagnating.

But the traditional Windsor is still very popular and is made in its thousands by the more traditional firms. Thomas Glenister was making Windsor chairs in 1839, and the firm's current catalogues can note that by 'using modern machinery and techniques where these can be applied, this enables us to produce these beautiful and graceful designs at prices within the reach of the majority'.

But there is still a select group of enthusiasts who seek out hand-made Windsor chairs, and these can still be found in the workshops of young craftsmen such as Stewart Linford at High Wycombe in Buckinghamshire. Here the bending of the bows is still done by steam and the saddling

Double-bow Windsor rocking chair designed by Lucian Ercolani and first produced by the High Wycome firm of Ercol Limited in 1962.

of the elm seats by use of the chairmaker's adze. The workmanship gives a genuine feel and finish to the chairs, which can be made to pattern and to measure.

Windsor chairs from the eighteenth century to the twentieth century are still sought-after items and rarities such as the writing arm chair, the double crest chair and the scarce Windsor settee can still excite the connoisseur. The enormous number of Windsor chairs made over the past 280 years of their development has made their acquisition still possible for the collector.

FURTHER READING

Cotton, B. D. *The English Regional Chair.* Antique Collectors' Club, 1990.
Crispin, T. *The English Windsor Chair.* Alan Sutton, 1992.
Evans, N. G. 'A History and Background of English Windsor Furniture' in *Furniture History,* volume 15 (1978), pages 24-53, plates 72-95.
Gloag, J. *The Englishman's Chair.* Allen & Unwin, 1964.
Knell, David. *English Country Furniture.* Shire, 1993.
Roe, F. G. *Windsor Chairs.* Phoenix House, 1953.
Sparkes, I. G. *The English Country Chair.* Spur Books, 1973.
Sparkes, I. G. *The Windsor Chair.* Spur Books, 1975.

A large number of articles have been published in magazines over the years covering the history of the Windsor chair, and a shortlist can be obtained from the Wycombe Local History and Chair Museum on request (see address below).

Research on the Windsor chair and other country furniture is now channelled through the Regional Furniture Society (membership: Gerry Cotton, Trouthouse, Warren's Cross, Lechlade, Gloucestershire), which produces a newsletter and annual publication and organises conferences, exhibitions and study sessions.

PLACES TO VISIT

Windsor chairs are frequently on display in houses open to the public, museums and craft centres. For specific collections, the reader is directed to the following museums:

Museum of English Rural Life, Whiteknights Park, Reading, Berkshire RG6 2AG. Telephone: 0734 318660.

Victoria and Albert Museum, Cromwell Road, South Kensington, London SW7 2RL. Telephone: 071-938 8500.

Welsh Folk Museum, St Fagans, Cardiff, South Glamorgan CF5 6XB. Telephone: 0222 569441.

Wycombe Local History and Chair Museum, Castle Hill House, Priory Avenue, High Wycombe, Buckinghamshire HP13 6PX. Telephone: 0494 421895.

ACKNOWLEDGEMENTS

I would like to acknowledge the help and advice received over the years from a wide circle of Windsor chair devotees, in particular to those who have provided me with photographs of unusual or significant chairs, and my thanks go especially to Laurie Stevens, Adrian Heath and his students of Arkitektskolen I Aarhus, the Victoria and Albert Museum, the Museum of English Rural Life, Dr Stabler, Parker Knoll Ltd, John H. Brandler, Stewart Linford and any other sources I may have omitted. In particular I must thank the Wycombe District Council for their support at Wycombe Chair Museum, where the collection of chairs and photographs have helped me pursue this interest. Photographs are acknowledged as follows: Ipswich Museum, page 28 (right); Museum of English Rural Life, pages 9 (bottom right), 23 (bottom right); Parker Knoll Collection, pages 6 (top right, bottom right), 12 (bottom right); Victoria and Albert Museum, pages 3 (left), 5 (left), 11 (left), 26 (right); Wycombe Chair Museum, pages 5 (right), 9 (bottom left), 11 (right), 15 (right), 18, 19 (top, bottom right), 20 (top left, bottom), 22 (top left, top right), 23 (top, bottom left), 24 (top right), 26 (bottom), 27 (right), 29 (right), 30 (both).